Self-Love Journal
Improve Your Mindset in 90 Days

Authors: Rebecca Norton and Jo Outram

Copyright © 2018 by Jo Outram.

All rights reserved. This book or any portion thereof may not be reproduced or used in any manner whatsoever without the express permission of the publisher or author except for the use of brief quotations in a book review or scholarly journal.

The published makes no representation, expressed or implied, with regards to the accuracy of the information contained in this book, and cannot accept any responsibility or liability. The comments made do not constitute professional advice.

First Printing: 2018

ISBN: 978-0-244-99804-2

Financial Fitness Instructor Ltd. South Yorkshire, S65
www.financialfitnessinstructor.co.uk

Printed in the UK

Self-Love Journal

Thank you for purchasing this self-love journal. Jo & I love that we can help you as you work towards improving your mindset around self-love.

I love using affirmations as they certainly have the feel-good factor, but if you want to really improve your mindset then you need to start re-programming your subconscious mind to allow you to believe that you are worthy. It is after all our subconscious mind that controls us in the background, taking us to places and situations that it believes we want.

The good news is that you can re-program your subconscious mind, by getting clear on what you want to achieve, examining how you will feel when you get to where you want to be, clearing the negative beliefs and then replacing them with positive ones (affirmations).

Follow the steps that we've laid out for you and try and complete the journal each day. Don't worry if you miss a day, just get right back into the process and keep moving forward.

Rebecca x

I'm delighted to share with you my five-step process for using affirmations and the Law of Attraction to help improve your mindset around self-love.

You might have used the Law of Attraction before, with mixed or no results. You are not alone. The main problem for the lack of results is that most people just ask, without being specific, and then give up when they do not receive!

First, the Law of Attraction does not always give results straight away. Giving up just cancels your order as the Universe thinks you no longer want what you have asked for. It is also difficult to manifest when you are coming from a place of desperation and don't belief in yourself.

Doubts are a big problem. These doubts (also referred to as limiting beliefs or blocks) are often buried in our subconscious mind. This is a problem as we act on these negative beliefs without even knowing we are doing this.

Follow the steps that we've included in the following pages and you'll be able to start using affirmations and the Law of Attraction to improve your mindset and start building the life you deserve (yes, you really do deserve everything that you desire).

Jo x

Step 1

You need to get super clear on what it is that you want out of your life, without putting any filters on your desires. You'll need to take some time to do this.

Find some quiet time, grab yourself a coffee, close the door, switch off all electronic distractions and think. You may want to meditate. A simple meditation will suffice.

Sit comfortably. You don't have to be sat in the floor in the lotus position, unless you are flexible enough for this to be comfortable. Sit in a comfortable chair if you prefer but sit without crossing your legs.

Close your eyes when it feels right to do so. Focus on your breathing by becoming aware of your abdomen as you breathe in and out. Just breathe normally.

Then when you feel ready, start to think about what self-love means to you?
If you were living the life that made you 100% happy, what would you be doing?
How would you be treating yourself?
How will your life be better when you are practicing self-love?

Then when you are ready, open your eyes and then start to journal on the thoughts that you have had. You might want to do this exercise several times until you are happy that you have captured all your thoughts.

Step 2

You are going to use positive affirmations to reinforce what you need to believe to be able to convince yourself that your are worthy.

Affirmations are words or phrases which you say repeatedly to affirm a thought about yourself. Thoughts that are repeated often enough soon become a belief.

Each day you should choose an affirmation to work with. Try to work through the process every day, but if you miss a day then don't beat yourself up, or even worse give up, just continue where you left off.

Some affirmations have been included in this journal, but feel free to write your own. If you do want to write your own, then just make sure that you write them in the present tense and that they are positive.

To use the ones provided here, just scan through the list (at the back of the journal) each day and see which one resonates with you and that's the one you need to work with for that day. If you are drawn to one, but instantly think that it is not right for you because ………. (just fill in the blank!) then it is probably a good idea to choose this affirmation, so you can work on dispelling the negativity it conjures up.

There are more than enough affirmations to cover all 90 days, but if you are drawn to an affirmation that you have used before, then use it again. It does not matter if use an affirmation more than once.

Write your affirmation in the box provided for each day. Write it out several times and say them to yourself in your head or out loud.

You need to do what makes you feel comfortable at the start of the 90 days. When you are ready to then you can say them out loud whilst looking at yourself in the mirror, but only do this when you feel ready to do so. By the end of 90 days, you should be getting comfortable enough to do this.

Step 3

When you start to doubt the affirmations that you have chosen, do not worry, it is just your subconscious mind sending a signal which is based on your current belief system. You do however need to work on getting rid of these doubts / negative beliefs / blocks.

Each day, when you are writing and saying your affirmation, take notice of any negative beliefs or doubts that you have and make a note of these in the journal. Space has been provided for you to do this. If you don't have any doubts then that's great, there is less work to do on that day!

Do you have doubts right now about not being able to accept self-love? If you do, then get them out into the open. I've left some space for you here to write them down. It's good for you to know what you are working against.

....
....
....
....
....
....
....
....
....
....
....
....

Step 4

You need to work on clearing your negative beliefs, so they don't stop you from believing in your positive affirmations and ultimately treating yourself in a loving way.

There are several ways you can work on clearing your negative beliefs, including using methods like EFT (emotional freedom technique), which can be very effective although outside the scope of this journal.

I love using the ancient Hawaiian prayer, known as Ho'oponopono Now, there is a fascinating story of how an Hawaiian Doctor cured a whole ward of criminally insane patients, by using Ho'oponopono and he did not even visit with any of the patients. I cannot recommend enough the book, Zero Limits by Dr Joe Vitale if you are intrigued to find out more.

The prayer is simply the following four phrases.

I'm sorry

Please forgive me

Thank you

I love you

I'm sorry This is our repentance. According to the Law of Attraction we are responsible for what our mind attracts to us, because we attract it, albeit on a sub-conscious level. Once you can accept this then it becomes very natural to feel sorry.

Please forgive me You need to say this and mean it. It does not matter who you are asking forgiveness from, whether it is yourself, the Universe or God. You are not however asking forgiveness from another person. You do not need their forgiveness.

Thank You This is a show of gratitude. Again, it does not matter who you are saying it to – yourself, the Universe, God. Just say it with feeling.

I love you Again it does not matter who you are saying it to – yourself, the Universe, God. Just say it with feeling.

You can say these phrases in any order.

You are going to use this prayer each day, by taking each doubt / negative belief in turn and saying the prayer several times. You can say the prayer to yourself anytime of the day, even without knowing what you are trying to clear.

Step 5

Finally, we are going to show gratitude.

If you are not doing so already, then a good habit to form is to show your gratitude for what you already have. Research has shown that writing down what we are grateful for has resulted in some impressive benefits.

You should not however just go through the motions. You should make a conscious decision to become more grateful, for the things around you, for the people in your life and the unexpected events. When writing what you are grateful for, you should try to use as much detail as possible. "I am grateful for the support I received from my family today, helping me deal with the problems I was having at work" is more meaningful than just "I am grateful for my family."

Some research has shown that it is best not to overdo it, when gratitude journaling, as writing daily can water down the benefits as we may start to find it difficult to genuinely feel gratitude. Of course, we are all different, so you should do what feels right, so long as you are writing regularly. If you feel writing daily is not for you, then write every other day, or three times a week. Timing is up to you. There is space each day for you to use, when it feels right for you.

Welcome to the beginning of your journey

**Self-Love Journal
Improve Your Mindset in 90 Days**

Day 1

Todays Affirmation:

Say this affirmation several times out loud with your hand on your heart looking at yourself in the mirror.

If you prefer to write it down, do that here.

1. ....
2. ....
3. ....
4. ....
5. ....

Date:

How does this affirmation make you feel?

....
....
....
....

What blocks/negative beliefs are brought up for you

....
....
....
....

Thinking of each block in turn, now say:
- *Please forgive me*
- *I'm sorry*
- *Thank you*
- *I love you*

Today I am grateful for:

....
....
....

Day 2

Todays Affirmation:

Say this affirmation several times out loud with your hand on your heart looking at yourself in the mirror.

If you prefer to write it down, do that here.

1. ....
2. ....
3. ....
4. ....
5. ....

Date:

How does this affirmation make you feel?

....

....

....

....

What blocks/negative beliefs are brought up for you

....

....

....

....

Thinking of each block in turn, now say:

- *Please forgive me*
- *I'm sorry*
- *Thank you*
- *I love you*

Today I am grateful for:

....

....

....

Day 3

Todays Affirmation:

Say this affirmation several times out loud with your hand on your heart looking at yourself in the mirror.

If you prefer to write it down, do that here.

1. ....
2. ....
3. ....
4. ....
5. ....

Date:

How does this affirmation make you feel?

....

....

....

....

What blocks/negative beliefs are brought up for you

....

....

....

....

Thinking of each block in turn, now say:

- *Please forgive me*
- *I'm sorry*
- *Thank you*
- *I love you*

Today I am grateful for:

....

....

....

Day 4

Todays Affirmation:

Say this affirmation several times out loud with your hand on your heart looking at yourself in the mirror.

If you prefer to write it down, do that here.

1. ....
2. ....
3. ....
4. ....
5. ....

Date:

How does this affirmation make you feel?

....

....

....

....

What blocks/negative beliefs are brought up for you

....

....

....

....

Thinking of each block in turn, now say:

- *Please forgive me*
- *I'm sorry*
- *Thank you*
- *I love you*

Today I am grateful for:

....

....

....

Day 5

Todays Affirmation:

Say this affirmation several times out loud with your hand on your heart looking at yourself in the mirror.

If you prefer to write it down, do that here.

1. ....
2. ....
3. ....
4. ....
5. ....

Date:

How does this affirmation make you feel?

....
....
....
....

What blocks/negative beliefs are brought up for you

....
....
....
....

Thinking of each block in turn, now say:

- *Please forgive me*
- *I'm sorry*
- *Thank you*
- *I love you*

Today I am grateful for:

....
....
....

Day 6

Todays Affirmation:

Say this affirmation several times out loud with your hand on your heart looking at yourself in the mirror.

If you prefer to write it down, do that here.

1. ....
2. ....
3. ....
4. ....
5. ....

Date:

How does this affirmation make you feel?

....

....

....

....

What blocks/negative beliefs are brought up for you

....

....

....

....

Thinking of each block in turn, now say:

- *Please forgive me*
- *I'm sorry*
- *Thank you*
- *I love you*

Today I am grateful for:

....

....

....

Day 7

Todays Affirmation:

Say this affirmation several times out loud with your hand on your heart looking at yourself in the mirror.

If you prefer to write it down, do that here.

1. ....
2. ....
3. ....
4. ....
5. ....

Date:
_____

How does this affirmation make you feel?

....

....

....

....

What blocks/negative beliefs are brought up for you

....

....

....

....

Thinking of each block in turn, now say:

- *Please forgive me*
- *I'm sorry*
- *Thank you*
- *I love you*

Today I am grateful for:

....

....

....

_____

Day 8

Todays Affirmation:

Say this affirmation several times out loud with your hand on your heart looking at yourself in the mirror.

If you prefer to write it down, do that here.

1. ....
2. ....
3. ....
4. ....
5. ....

Date:

How does this affirmation make you feel?

....
....
....
....

What blocks/negative beliefs are brought up for you

....
....
....
....

Thinking of each block in turn, now say:
- *Please forgive me*
- *I'm sorry*
- *Thank you*
- *I love you*

Today I am grateful for:

....
....
....

Day 9

Todays Affirmation:

Say this affirmation several times out loud with your hand on your heart looking at yourself in the mirror.

If you prefer to write it down, do that here.

1. ....
2. ....
3. ....
4. ....
5. ....

Date:

How does this affirmation make you feel?

....
....
....
....

What blocks/negative beliefs are brought up for you

....
....
....
....

Thinking of each block in turn, now say:

- *Please forgive me*
- *I'm sorry*
- *Thank you*
- *I love you*

Today I am grateful for:

....
....
....

Day 10

Todays Affirmation:

Say this affirmation several times out loud with your hand on your heart looking at yourself in the mirror.

If you prefer to write it down, do that here.

1. ....
2. ....
3. ....
4. ....
5. ....

Date:

How does this affirmation make you feel?

....

....

....

....

What blocks/negative beliefs are brought up for you

....

....

....

....

Thinking of each block in turn, now say:
- *Please forgive me*
- *I'm sorry*
- *Thank you*
- *I love you*

Today I am grateful for:

....

....

....

Day 11

Todays Affirmation:

Say this affirmation several times out loud with your hand on your heart looking at yourself in the mirror.

If you prefer to write it down, do that here.

1. ....
2. ....
3. ....
4. ....
5. ....

Date:

How does this affirmation make you feel?

....

....

....

....

What blocks/negative beliefs are brought up for you

....

....

....

....

Thinking of each block in turn, now say:
- *Please forgive me*
- *I'm sorry*
- *Thank you*
- *I love you*

Today I am grateful for:

....

....

....

Day 12

Todays Affirmation:

Say this affirmation several times out loud with your hand on your heart looking at yourself in the mirror.

If you prefer to write it down, do that here.

1. ....
2. ....
3. ....
4. ....
5. ....

Date:

How does this affirmation make you feel?

....

....

....

....

What blocks/negative beliefs are brought up for you

....

....

....

....

Thinking of each block in turn, now say:

- *Please forgive me*
- *I'm sorry*
- *Thank you*
- *I love you*

Today I am grateful for:

....

....

....

Day 13

Todays Affirmation:

Say this affirmation several times out loud with your hand on your heart looking at yourself in the mirror.

If you prefer to write it down, do that here.

1. ....
2. ....
3. ....
4. ....
5. ....

Date:

How does this affirmation make you feel?

....

....

....

....

What blocks/negative beliefs are brought up for you

....

....

....

....

Thinking of each block in turn, now say:
- *Please forgive me*
- *I'm sorry*
- *Thank you*
- *I love you*

Today I am grateful for:

....

....

....

Day 14

Todays Affirmation:

Say this affirmation several times out loud with your hand on your heart looking at yourself in the mirror.

If you prefer to write it down, do that here.

1. ....
2. ....
3. ....
4. ....
5. ....

Date:
_____

How does this affirmation make you feel?

....

....

....

....

What blocks/negative beliefs are brought up for you

....

....

....

....

Thinking of each block in turn, now say:
- *Please forgive me*
- *I'm sorry*
- *Thank you*
- *I love you*

Today I am grateful for:

....

....

....
_____

Day 15

Todays Affirmation:

Say this affirmation several times out loud with your hand on your heart looking at yourself in the mirror.

If you prefer to write it down, do that here.

1. ....
2. ....
3. ....
4. ....
5. ....

Date:

How does this affirmation make you feel?

....

....

....

....

What blocks/negative beliefs are brought up for you

....

....

....

....

Thinking of each block in turn, now say:

- *Please forgive me*
- *I'm sorry*
- *Thank you*
- *I love you*

Today I am grateful for:

....

....

....

Day 16

Todays Affirmation:

Say this affirmation several times out loud with your hand on your heart looking at yourself in the mirror.

If you prefer to write it down, do that here.

1. ....
2. ....
3. ....
4. ....
5. ....

Date:

How does this affirmation make you feel?

....
....
....
....

What blocks/negative beliefs are brought up for you

....
....
....
....

Thinking of each block in turn, now say:
- *Please forgive me*
- *I'm sorry*
- *Thank you*
- *I love you*

Today I am grateful for:

....
....
....

Day 17

Todays Affirmation:

Say this affirmation several times out loud with your hand on your heart looking at yourself in the mirror.

If you prefer to write it down, do that here.

1. ....
2. ....
3. ....
4. ....
5. ....

Date:

How does this affirmation make you feel?

....
....
....
....

What blocks/negative beliefs are brought up for you

....
....
....
....

Thinking of each block in turn, now say:
- *Please forgive me*
- *I'm sorry*
- *Thank you*
- *I love you*

Today I am grateful for:

....
....
....

Day 18

Todays Affirmation:

Say this affirmation several times out loud with your hand on your heart looking at yourself in the mirror.

If you prefer to write it down, do that here.

1. ....
2. ....
3. ....
4. ....
5. ....

Date:

How does this affirmation make you feel?

....
....
....
....

What blocks/negative beliefs are brought up for you

....
....
....
....

Thinking of each block in turn, now say:

- *Please forgive me*
- *I'm sorry*
- *Thank you*
- *I love you*

Today I am grateful for:

....
....
....

Day 19

Todays Affirmation:

Say this affirmation several times out loud with your hand on your heart looking at yourself in the mirror.

If you prefer to write it down, do that here.

1. ....
2. ....
3. ....
4. ....
5. ....

Date:

How does this affirmation make you feel?

....

....

....

....

What blocks/negative beliefs are brought up for you

....

....

....

....

Thinking of each block in turn, now say:
- *Please forgive me*
- *I'm sorry*
- *Thank you*
- *I love you*

Today I am grateful for:

....

....

....

Day 20

Todays Affirmation:

Say this affirmation several times out loud with your hand on your heart looking at yourself in the mirror.

If you prefer to write it down, do that here.

1. ....
2. ....
3. ....
4. ....
5. ....

Date:

How does this affirmation make you feel?

....

....

....

....

What blocks/negative beliefs are brought up for you

....

....

....

....

Thinking of each block in turn, now say:

- *Please forgive me*
- *I'm sorry*
- *Thank you*
- *I love you*

Today I am grateful for:

....

....

....

Day 21

Todays Affirmation:

Say this affirmation several times out loud with your hand on your heart looking at yourself in the mirror.

If you prefer to write it down, do that here.

1. ....
2. ....
3. ....
4. ....
5. ....

Date:

How does this affirmation make you feel?

....

....

....

....

What blocks/negative beliefs are brought up for you

....

....

....

....

Thinking of each block in turn, now say:

- *Please forgive me*
- *I'm sorry*
- *Thank you*
- *I love you*

Today I am grateful for:

....

....

....

Day 22

Todays Affirmation:

Say this affirmation several times out loud with your hand on your heart looking at yourself in the mirror.

If you prefer to write it down, do that here.

1. ....
2. ....
3. ....
4. ....
5. ....

Date:

How does this affirmation make you feel?

....

....

....

....

What blocks/negative beliefs are brought up for you

....

....

....

....

Thinking of each block in turn, now say:
- *Please forgive me*
- *I'm sorry*
- *Thank you*
- *I love you*

Today I am grateful for:

....

....

....

Day 23

Todays Affirmation:

Say this affirmation several times out loud with your hand on your heart looking at yourself in the mirror.

If you prefer to write it down, do that here.

1. ....
2. ....
3. ....
4. ....
5. ....

Date:

How does this affirmation make you feel?

....

....

....

....

What blocks/negative beliefs are brought up for you

....

....

....

....

Thinking of each block in turn, now say:
- *Please forgive me*
- *I'm sorry*
- *Thank you*
- *I love you*

Today I am grateful for:

....

....

....

Day 24

Todays Affirmation:

Say this affirmation several times out loud with your hand on your heart looking at yourself in the mirror.

If you prefer to write it down, do that here.

1. ....
2. ....
3. ....
4. ....
5. ....

Date:

How does this affirmation make you feel?

....
....
....
....

What blocks/negative beliefs are brought up for you

....
....
....
....

Thinking of each block in turn, now say:
- *Please forgive me*
- *I'm sorry*
- *Thank you*
- *I love you*

Today I am grateful for:

....
....
....

Day 25

Todays Affirmation:

Say this affirmation several times out loud with your hand on your heart looking at yourself in the mirror.

If you prefer to write it down, do that here.

1. ....
2. ....
3. ....
4. ....
5. ....

Date:

How does this affirmation make you feel?

....
....
....
....

What blocks/negative beliefs are brought up for you

....
....
....
....

Thinking of each block in turn, now say:
- *Please forgive me*
- *I'm sorry*
- *Thank you*
- *I love you*

Today I am grateful for:

....
....
....

Day 26

Todays Affirmation:

Say this affirmation several times out loud with your hand on your heart looking at yourself in the mirror.

If you prefer to write it down, do that here.

1. ....
2. ....
3. ....
4. ....
5. ....

Date:

How does this affirmation make you feel?

....

....

....

....

What blocks/negative beliefs are brought up for you

....

....

....

....

Thinking of each block in turn, now say:
- *Please forgive me*
- *I'm sorry*
- *Thank you*
- *I love you*

Today I am grateful for:

....

....

....

Day 27

Todays Affirmation:

Say this affirmation several times out loud with your hand on your heart looking at yourself in the mirror.

If you prefer to write it down, do that here.

1. ....
2. ....
3. ....
4. ....
5. ....

Date:
_____

How does this affirmation make you feel?

....

....

....

....

What blocks/negative beliefs are brought up for you

....

....

....

....

Thinking of each block in turn, now say:

- *Please forgive me*
- *I'm sorry*
- *Thank you*
- *I love you*

Today I am grateful for:

....

....

....

_____

Day 28

Todays Affirmation:

Say this affirmation several times out loud with your hand on your heart looking at yourself in the mirror.

If you prefer to write it down, do that here.

1. ....
2. ....
3. ....
4. ....
5. ....

Date:

How does this affirmation make you feel?

....

....

....

....

What blocks/negative beliefs are brought up for you

....

....

....

....

Thinking of each block in turn, now say:
- *Please forgive me*
- *I'm sorry*
- *Thank you*
- *I love you*

Today I am grateful for:

....

....

....

Day 29

Todays Affirmation:

Say this affirmation several times out loud with your hand on your heart looking at yourself in the mirror.

If you prefer to write it down, do that here.

1. ....
2. ....
3. ....
4. ....
5. ....

Date:

How does this affirmation make you feel?

....

....

....

....

What blocks/negative beliefs are brought up for you

....

....

....

....

Thinking of each block in turn, now say:

- *Please forgive me*
- *I'm sorry*
- *Thank you*
- *I love you*

Today I am grateful for:

....

....

....

Day 30

Todays Affirmation:

Say this affirmation several times out loud with your hand on your heart looking at yourself in the mirror.

If you prefer to write it down, do that here.

1. ....
2. ....
3. ....
4. ....
5. ....

Date:

How does this affirmation make you feel?

....

....

....

....

What blocks/negative beliefs are brought up for you

....

....

....

....

Thinking of each block in turn, now say:

- *Please forgive me*
- *I'm sorry*
- *Thank you*
- *I love you*

Today I am grateful for:

....

....

....

How do I feel my mindset has improved over the last 30 days?

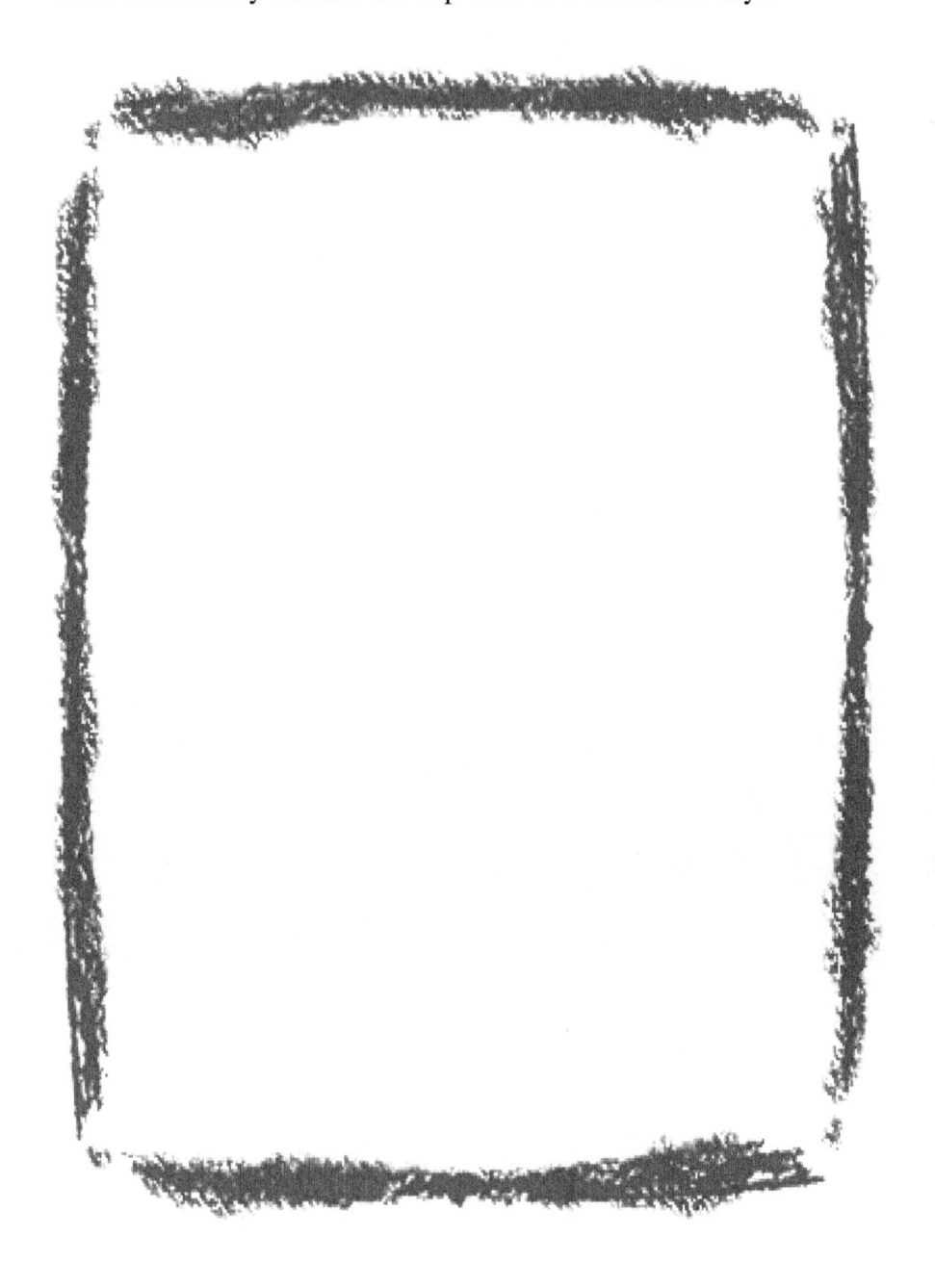

How do I want the Universe to guide me in the next 30 days?

Day 31

Todays Affirmation:

Say this affirmation several times out loud with your hand on your heart looking at yourself in the mirror.

If you prefer to write it down, do that here.

1. ....
2. ....
3. ....
4. ....
5. ....

Date:

How does this affirmation make you feel?

....
....
....
....

What blocks/negative beliefs are brought up for you

....
....
....
....

Thinking of each block in turn, now say:
- *Please forgive me*
- *I'm sorry*
- *Thank you*
- *I love you*

Today I am grateful for:

....
....
....

Day 32

Todays Affirmation:

Say this affirmation several times out loud with your hand on your heart looking at yourself in the mirror.

If you prefer to write it down, do that here.

1. ....
2. ....
3. ....
4. ....
5. ....

Date:

How does this affirmation make you feel?

....
....
....
....

What blocks/negative beliefs are brought up for you

....
....
....
....

Thinking of each block in turn, now say:

- *Please forgive me*
- *I'm sorry*
- *Thank you*
- *I love you*

Today I am grateful for:

....
....
....

Day 33

Todays Affirmation:

Say this affirmation several times out loud with your hand on your heart looking at yourself in the mirror.

If you prefer to write it down, do that here.

1. ....
2. ....
3. ....
4. ....
5. ....

Date:

How does this affirmation make you feel?

....
....
....
....

What blocks/negative beliefs are brought up for you

....
....
....
....

Thinking of each block in turn, now say:
- *Please forgive me*
- *I'm sorry*
- *Thank you*
- *I love you*

Today I am grateful for:

....
....
....

Day 34

Todays Affirmation:

Say this affirmation several times out loud with your hand on your heart looking at yourself in the mirror.

If you prefer to write it down, do that here.

1. ....
2. ....
3. ....
4. ....
5. ....

Date:

How does this affirmation make you feel?

....
....
....
....

What blocks/negative beliefs are brought up for you

....
....
....
....

Thinking of each block in turn, now say:
- *Please forgive me*
- *I'm sorry*
- *Thank you*
- *I love you*

Today I am grateful for:

....
....
....

Day 35

Todays Affirmation:

Say this affirmation several times out loud with your hand on your heart looking at yourself in the mirror.

If you prefer to write it down, do that here.

1. ....
2. ....
3. ....
4. ....
5. ....

Date:

How does this affirmation make you feel?
....
....
....
....

What blocks/negative beliefs are brought up for you
....
....
....
....

Thinking of each block in turn, now say:
- *Please forgive me*
- *I'm sorry*
- *Thank you*
- *I love you*

Today I am grateful for:
....
....
....

Day 36

Todays Affirmation:

Say this affirmation several times out loud with your hand on your heart looking at yourself in the mirror.

If you prefer to write it down, do that here.

1. ....
2. ....
3. ....
4. ....
5. ....

Date:

How does this affirmation make you feel?

....
....
....
....

What blocks/negative beliefs are brought up for you

....
....
....
....

Thinking of each block in turn, now say:

- *Please forgive me*
- *I'm sorry*
- *Thank you*
- *I love you*

Today I am grateful for:

....
....
....

Day 37

Todays Affirmation:

Say this affirmation several times out loud with your hand on your heart looking at yourself in the mirror.

If you prefer to write it down, do that here.

1. ....
2. ....
3. ....
4. ....
5. ....

Date:

How does this affirmation make you feel?

....
....
....
....

What blocks/negative beliefs are brought up for you

....
....
....
....

Thinking of each block in turn, now say:

- *Please forgive me*
- *I'm sorry*
- *Thank you*
- *I love you*

Today I am grateful for:

....
....
....

Day 38

Todays Affirmation:

Say this affirmation several times out loud with your hand on your heart looking at yourself in the mirror.

If you prefer to write it down, do that here.

1. ....
2. ....
3. ....
4. ....
5. ....

Date:

How does this affirmation make you feel?

....
....
....
....

What blocks/negative beliefs are brought up for you

....
....
....
....

Thinking of each block in turn, now say:

- *Please forgive me*
- *I'm sorry*
- *Thank you*
- *I love you*

Today I am grateful for:

....
....
....

Day 39

Todays Affirmation:

Say this affirmation several times out loud with your hand on your heart looking at yourself in the mirror.

If you prefer to write it down, do that here.

1. ....
2. ....
3. ....
4. ....
5. ....

Date:

How does this affirmation make you feel?

....

....

....

....

What blocks/negative beliefs are brought up for you

....

....

....

....

Thinking of each block in turn, now say:
- *Please forgive me*
- *I'm sorry*
- *Thank you*
- *I love you*

Today I am grateful for:

....

....

....

Day 40

Todays Affirmation:

Say this affirmation several times out loud with your hand on your heart looking at yourself in the mirror.

If you prefer to write it down, do that here.

1. ....
2. ....
3. ....
4. ....
5. ....

Date:

How does this affirmation make you feel?

....

....

....

....

What blocks/negative beliefs are brought up for you

....

....

....

....

Thinking of each block in turn, now say:

- *Please forgive me*
- *I'm sorry*
- *Thank you*
- *I love you*

Today I am grateful for:

....

....

....

Day 41

Todays Affirmation:

Say this affirmation several times out loud with your hand on your heart looking at yourself in the mirror.

If you prefer to write it down, do that here.

1. ....
2. ....
3. ....
4. ....
5. ....

Date:

How does this affirmation make you feel?

....

....

....

....

What blocks/negative beliefs are brought up for you

....

....

....

....

Thinking of each block in turn, now say:

- *Please forgive me*
- *I'm sorry*
- *Thank you*
- *I love you*

Today I am grateful for:

....

....

....

Day 42

Todays Affirmation:

Say this affirmation several times out loud with your hand on your heart looking at yourself in the mirror.

If you prefer to write it down, do that here.

1. ....
2. ....
3. ....
4. ....
5. ....

Date:

How does this affirmation make you feel?

....
....
....
....

What blocks/negative beliefs are brought up for you

....
....
....
....

Thinking of each block in turn, now say:
- *Please forgive me*
- *I'm sorry*
- *Thank you*
- *I love you*

Today I am grateful for:

....
....
....

Day 43

Todays Affirmation:

Say this affirmation several times out loud with your hand on your heart looking at yourself in the mirror.

If you prefer to write it down, do that here.

1. ....
2. ....
3. ....
4. ....
5. ....

Date:

How does this affirmation make you feel?

....
....
....
....

What blocks/negative beliefs are brought up for you

....
....
....
....

Thinking of each block in turn, now say:

- *Please forgive me*
- *I'm sorry*
- *Thank you*
- *I love you*

Today I am grateful for:

....
....
....

Day 44

Todays Affirmation:

Say this affirmation several times out loud with your hand on your heart looking at yourself in the mirror.

If you prefer to write it down, do that here.

1. ....
2. ....
3. ....
4. ....
5. ....

Date:

How does this affirmation make you feel?

....

....

....

....

What blocks/negative beliefs are brought up for you

....

....

....

....

Thinking of each block in turn, now say:

- *Please forgive me*
- *I'm sorry*
- *Thank you*
- *I love you*

Today I am grateful for:

....

....

....

Day 45

Todays Affirmation:

Say this affirmation several times out loud with your hand on your heart looking at yourself in the mirror.

If you prefer to write it down, do that here.

1. ....
2. ....
3. ....
4. ....
5. ....

Date:

How does this affirmation make you feel?

....

....

....

....

What blocks/negative beliefs are brought up for you

....

....

....

....

Thinking of each block in turn, now say:
- *Please forgive me*
- *I'm sorry*
- *Thank you*
- *I love you*

Today I am grateful for:

....

....

....

Day 46

Todays Affirmation:

Say this affirmation several times out loud with your hand on your heart looking at yourself in the mirror.

If you prefer to write it down, do that here.

1. ....
2. ....
3. ....
4. ....
5. ....

Date:

How does this affirmation make you feel?

....

....

....

....

What blocks/negative beliefs are brought up for you

....

....

....

....

Thinking of each block in turn, now say:
- *Please forgive me*
- *I'm sorry*
- *Thank you*
- *I love you*

Today I am grateful for:

....

....

....

Day 47

Todays Affirmation:

Say this affirmation several times out loud with your hand on your heart looking at yourself in the mirror.

If you prefer to write it down, do that here.

1. ....
2. ....
3. ....
4. ....
5. ....

Date:

How does this affirmation make you feel?

....

....

....

....

What blocks/negative beliefs are brought up for you

....

....

....

....

Thinking of each block in turn, now say:

- *Please forgive me*
- *I'm sorry*
- *Thank you*
- *I love you*

Today I am grateful for:

....

....

....

Day 48

Todays Affirmation:

Say this affirmation several times out loud with your hand on your heart looking at yourself in the mirror.

If you prefer to write it down, do that here.

1. ....
2. ....
3. ....
4. ....
5. ....

Date:

How does this affirmation make you feel?

....

....

....

....

What blocks/negative beliefs are brought up for you

....

....

....

....

Thinking of each block in turn, now say:
- *Please forgive me*
- *I'm sorry*
- *Thank you*
- *I love you*

Today I am grateful for:

....

....

....

Day 49

Todays Affirmation:

Say this affirmation several times out loud with your hand on your heart looking at yourself in the mirror.

If you prefer to write it down, do that here.

1. ....
2. ....
3. ....
4. ....
5. ....

Date:
_____

How does this affirmation make you feel?

....

....

....

....

What blocks/negative beliefs are brought up for you

....

....

....

....

Thinking of each block in turn, now say:
- *Please forgive me*
- *I'm sorry*
- *Thank you*
- *I love you*

Today I am grateful for:

....

....

....

_____

Day 50

Todays Affirmation:

Say this affirmation several times out loud with your hand on your heart looking at yourself in the mirror.

If you prefer to write it down, do that here.

1. ....
2. ....
3. ....
4. ....
5. ....

Date:

How does this affirmation make you feel?

....
....
....
....

What blocks/negative beliefs are brought up for you

....
....
....
....

Thinking of each block in turn, now say:

- *Please forgive me*
- *I'm sorry*
- *Thank you*
- *I love you*

Today I am grateful for:

....
....
....

Day 51

Todays Affirmation:

Say this affirmation several times out loud with your hand on your heart looking at yourself in the mirror.

If you prefer to write it down, do that here.

1. ....
2. ....
3. ....
4. ....
5. ....

Date:

How does this affirmation make you feel?

....
....
....
....

What blocks/negative beliefs are brought up for you

....
....
....
....

Thinking of each block in turn, now say:
- *Please forgive me*
- *I'm sorry*
- *Thank you*
- *I love you*

Today I am grateful for:

....
....
....

Day 52

Todays Affirmation:

Say this affirmation several times out loud with your hand on your heart looking at yourself in the mirror.

If you prefer to write it down, do that here.

1. ....
2. ....
3. ....
4. ....
5. ....

Date:
_____

How does this affirmation make you feel?

....

....

....

....

What blocks/negative beliefs are brought up for you

....

....

....

....

Thinking of each block in turn, now say:

- *Please forgive me*
- *I'm sorry*
- *Thank you*
- *I love you*

Today I am grateful for:

....

....

....

_____

Day 53

Todays Affirmation:

Say this affirmation several times out loud with your hand on your heart looking at yourself in the mirror.

If you prefer to write it down, do that here.

1. ....
2. ....
3. ....
4. ....
5. ....

Date:

How does this affirmation make you feel?

....
....
....
....

What blocks/negative beliefs are brought up for you

....
....
....
....

Thinking of each block in turn, now say:

- *Please forgive me*
- *I'm sorry*
- *Thank you*
- *I love you*

Today I am grateful for:

....
....
....

Day 54

Todays Affirmation:

Say this affirmation several times out loud with your hand on your heart looking at yourself in the mirror.

If you prefer to write it down, do that here.

1. ....
2. ....
3. ....
4. ....
5. ....

Date:
_____

How does this affirmation make you feel?

....

....

....

....

What blocks/negative beliefs are brought up for you

....

....

....

....

Thinking of each block in turn, now say:

- *Please forgive me*
- *I'm sorry*
- *Thank you*
- *I love you*

Today I am grateful for:

....

....

....
_____

Day 55

Todays Affirmation:

Say this affirmation several times out loud with your hand on your heart looking at yourself in the mirror.

If you prefer to write it down, do that here.

1. ....
2. ....
3. ....
4. ....
5. ....

Date:

How does this affirmation make you feel?

....
....
....
....

What blocks/negative beliefs are brought up for you

....
....
....
....

Thinking of each block in turn, now say:
- *Please forgive me*
- *I'm sorry*
- *Thank you*
- *I love you*

Today I am grateful for:

....
....
....

Day 56

Todays Affirmation:

Say this affirmation several times out loud with your hand on your heart looking at yourself in the mirror.

If you prefer to write it down, do that here.

1. ....
2. ....
3. ....
4. ....
5. ....

Date:

How does this affirmation make you feel?

....
....
....
....

What blocks/negative beliefs are brought up for you

....
....
....
....

Thinking of each block in turn, now say:

- *Please forgive me*
- *I'm sorry*
- *Thank you*
- *I love you*

Today I am grateful for:

....
....
....

Day 57

Todays Affirmation:

Say this affirmation several times out loud with your hand on your heart looking at yourself in the mirror.

If you prefer to write it down, do that here.

1. ....
2. ....
3. ....
4. ....
5. ....

Date:

How does this affirmation make you feel?

....

....

....

....

What blocks/negative beliefs are brought up for you

....

....

....

....

Thinking of each block in turn, now say:
- *Please forgive me*
- *I'm sorry*
- *Thank you*
- *I love you*

Today I am grateful for:

....

....

....

Day 58

Todays Affirmation:

Say this affirmation several times out loud with your hand on your heart looking at yourself in the mirror.

If you prefer to write it down, do that here.

1. ....
2. ....
3. ....
4. ....
5. ....

Date:
_____

How does this affirmation make you feel?

....

....

....

....

What blocks/negative beliefs are brought up for you

....

....

....

....

Thinking of each block in turn, now say:
- *Please forgive me*
- *I'm sorry*
- *Thank you*
- *I love you*

Today I am grateful for:

....

....

....

_____

Day 59

Todays Affirmation:

Say this affirmation several times out loud with your hand on your heart looking at yourself in the mirror.

If you prefer to write it down, do that here.

1. ....
2. ....
3. ....
4. ....
5. ....

Date:

How does this affirmation make you feel?

....

....

....

....

What blocks/negative beliefs are brought up for you

....

....

....

....

Thinking of each block in turn, now say:

- *Please forgive me*
- *I'm sorry*
- *Thank you*
- *I love you*

Today I am grateful for:

....

....

....

Day 60

Todays Affirmation:

Say this affirmation several times out loud with your hand on your heart looking at yourself in the mirror.

If you prefer to write it down, do that here.

1. ....
2. ....
3. ....
4. ....
5. ....

Date:

How does this affirmation make you feel?

....

....

....

....

What blocks/negative beliefs are brought up for you

....

....

....

....

Thinking of each block in turn, now say:
- *Please forgive me*
- *I'm sorry*
- *Thank you*
- *I love you*

Today I am grateful for:

....

....

....

How do I feel my mindset has improved over the last 30 days?

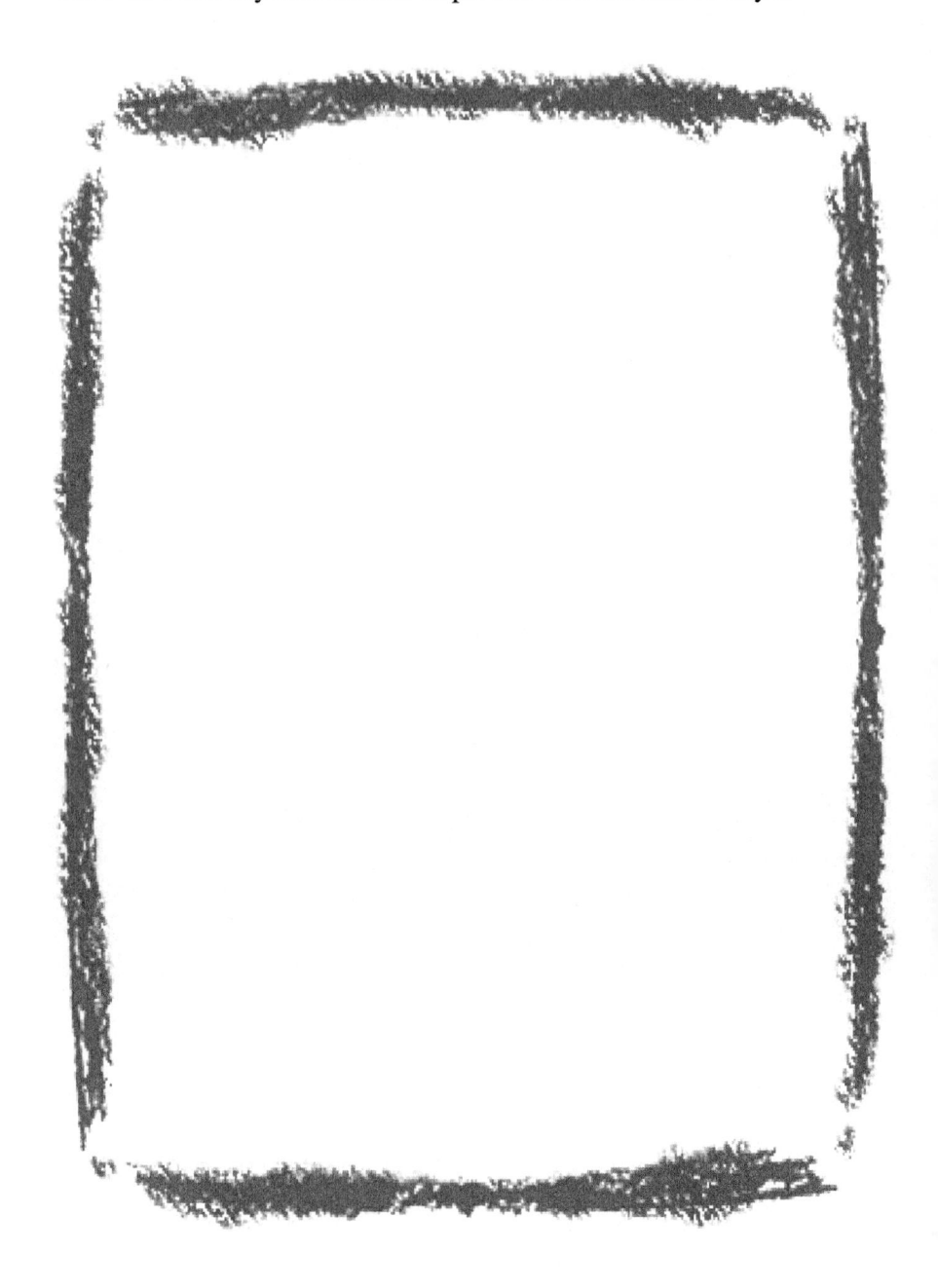

How do I want the Universe to guide me in the next 30 days?

Day 61

Todays Affirmation:

Say this affirmation several times out loud with your hand on your heart looking at yourself in the mirror.

If you prefer to write it down, do that here.

1. ....
2. ....
3. ....
4. ....
5. ....

Date:

How does this affirmation make you feel?

....

....

....

....

What blocks/negative beliefs are brought up for you

....

....

....

....

Thinking of each block in turn, now say:

- *Please forgive me*
- *I'm sorry*
- *Thank you*
- *I love you*

Today I am grateful for:

....

....

....

Day 62

Todays Affirmation:

Say this affirmation several times out loud with your hand on your heart looking at yourself in the mirror.

If you prefer to write it down, do that here.

1. ....
2. ....
3. ....
4. ....
5. ....

Date:

How does this affirmation make you feel?

....

....

....

....

What blocks/negative beliefs are brought up for you

....

....

....

....

Thinking of each block in turn, now say:
- *Please forgive me*
- *I'm sorry*
- *Thank you*
- *I love you*

Today I am grateful for:

....

....

....

Day 63

Todays Affirmation:

Say this affirmation several times out loud with your hand on your heart looking at yourself in the mirror.

If you prefer to write it down, do that here.

1. ....
2. ....
3. ....
4. ....
5. ....

Date:

How does this affirmation make you feel?

....
....
....
....

What blocks/negative beliefs are brought up for you

....
....
....
....

Thinking of each block in turn, now say:
- *Please forgive me*
- *I'm sorry*
- *Thank you*
- *I love you*

Today I am grateful for:

....
....
....

Day 64

Todays Affirmation:

Say this affirmation several times out loud with your hand on your heart looking at yourself in the mirror.

If you prefer to write it down, do that here.

1. ....
2. ....
3. ....
4. ....
5. ....

Date:

How does this affirmation make you feel?

....

....

....

....

What blocks/negative beliefs are brought up for you

....

....

....

....

Thinking of each block in turn, now say:

- *Please forgive me*
- *I'm sorry*
- *Thank you*
- *I love you*

Today I am grateful for:

....

....

....

Day 65

Todays Affirmation:

Say this affirmation several times out loud with your hand on your heart looking at yourself in the mirror.

If you prefer to write it down, do that here.

1. ....
2. ....
3. ....
4. ....
5. ....

Date:

How does this affirmation make you feel?

....

....

....

....

What blocks/negative beliefs are brought up for you

....

....

....

....

Thinking of each block in turn, now say:

- *Please forgive me*
- *I'm sorry*
- *Thank you*
- *I love you*

Today I am grateful for:

....

....

....

Day 66

Todays Affirmation:

Say this affirmation several times out loud with your hand on your heart looking at yourself in the mirror.

If you prefer to write it down, do that here.

1. ....
2. ....
3. ....
4. ....
5. ....

Date:

How does this affirmation make you feel?

....
....
....
....

What blocks/negative beliefs are brought up for you

....
....
....
....

Thinking of each block in turn, now say:
- *Please forgive me*
- *I'm sorry*
- *Thank you*
- *I love you*

Today I am grateful for:

....
....
....

Day 67

Todays Affirmation:

Say this affirmation several times out loud with your hand on your heart looking at yourself in the mirror.

If you prefer to write it down, do that here.

1. ....
2. ....
3. ....
4. ....
5. ....

Date:

How does this affirmation make you feel?

....

....

....

....

What blocks/negative beliefs are brought up for you

....

....

....

....

Thinking of each block in turn, now say:

- *Please forgive me*
- *I'm sorry*
- *Thank you*
- *I love you*

Today I am grateful for:

....

....

....

Day 68

Todays Affirmation:

Say this affirmation several times out loud with your hand on your heart looking at yourself in the mirror.

If you prefer to write it down, do that here.

1. ....
2. ....
3. ....
4. ....
5. ....

Date:
_____

How does this affirmation make you feel?

....

....

....

....

What blocks/negative beliefs are brought up for you

....

....

....

....

Thinking of each block in turn, now say:
- *Please forgive me*
- *I'm sorry*
- *Thank you*
- *I love you*

Today I am grateful for:

....

....

....

_____

Day 69

Todays Affirmation:

Say this affirmation several times out loud with your hand on your heart looking at yourself in the mirror.

If you prefer to write it down, do that here.

1. ....
2. ....
3. ....
4. ....
5. ....

Date:

How does this affirmation make you feel?

....

....

....

....

What blocks/negative beliefs are brought up for you

....

....

....

....

Thinking of each block in turn, now say:
- *Please forgive me*
- *I'm sorry*
- *Thank you*
- *I love you*

Today I am grateful for:

....

....

....

Day 70

Todays Affirmation:

Say this affirmation several times out loud with your hand on your heart looking at yourself in the mirror.

If you prefer to write it down, do that here.

1. ....
2. ....
3. ....
4. ....
5. ....

Date:

How does this affirmation make you feel?

....
....
....
....

What blocks/negative beliefs are brought up for you

....
....
....
....

Thinking of each block in turn, now say:

- *Please forgive me*
- *I'm sorry*
- *Thank you*
- *I love you*

Today I am grateful for:

....
....
....

Day 71

Todays Affirmation:

Say this affirmation several times out loud with your hand on your heart looking at yourself in the mirror.

If you prefer to write it down, do that here.

1. ....
2. ....
3. ....
4. ....
5. ....

Date:

How does this affirmation make you feel?

....

....

....

....

What blocks/negative beliefs are brought up for you

....

....

....

....

Thinking of each block in turn, now say:
- *Please forgive me*
- *I'm sorry*
- *Thank you*
- *I love you*

Today I am grateful for:

....

....

....

Day 72

Todays Affirmation:

Say this affirmation several times out loud with your hand on your heart looking at yourself in the mirror.

If you prefer to write it down, do that here.

1. ....
2. ....
3. ....
4. ....
5. ....

Date:

How does this affirmation make you feel?

....

....

....

....

What blocks/negative beliefs are brought up for you

....

....

....

....

Thinking of each block in turn, now say:

- *Please forgive me*
- *I'm sorry*
- *Thank you*
- *I love you*

Today I am grateful for:

....

....

....

Day 73

Todays Affirmation:

Say this affirmation several times out loud with your hand on your heart looking at yourself in the mirror.

If you prefer to write it down, do that here.

1. ....
2. ....
3. ....
4. ....
5. ....

Date:

How does this affirmation make you feel?

....

....

....

....

What blocks/negative beliefs are brought up for you

....

....

....

....

Thinking of each block in turn, now say:

- *Please forgive me*
- *I'm sorry*
- *Thank you*
- *I love you*

Today I am grateful for:

....

....

....

Day 74

Todays Affirmation:

Say this affirmation several times out loud with your hand on your heart looking at yourself in the mirror.

If you prefer to write it down, do that here.

1. ....
2. ....
3. ....
4. ....
5. ....

Date:

How does this affirmation make you feel?

....

....

....

....

What blocks/negative beliefs are brought up for you

....

....

....

....

Thinking of each block in turn, now say:

- *Please forgive me*
- *I'm sorry*
- *Thank you*
- *I love you*

Today I am grateful for:

....

....

....

Day 75

Todays Affirmation:

Say this affirmation several times out loud with your hand on your heart looking at yourself in the mirror.

If you prefer to write it down, do that here.

1. ....
2. ....
3. ....
4. ....
5. ....

Date:

How does this affirmation make you feel?

....

....

....

....

What blocks/negative beliefs are brought up for you

....

....

....

....

Thinking of each block in turn, now say:

- *Please forgive me*
- *I'm sorry*
- *Thank you*
- *I love you*

Today I am grateful for:

....

....

....

Day 76

Todays Affirmation:

Say this affirmation several times out loud with your hand on your heart looking at yourself in the mirror.

If you prefer to write it down, do that here.

1. ....
2. ....
3. ....
4. ....
5. ....

Date:

How does this affirmation make you feel?

....
....
....
....

What blocks/negative beliefs are brought up for you

....
....
....
....

Thinking of each block in turn, now say:

- *Please forgive me*
- *I'm sorry*
- *Thank you*
- *I love you*

Today I am grateful for:

....
....
....

Day 77

Todays Affirmation:

Say this affirmation several times out loud with your hand on your heart looking at yourself in the mirror.

If you prefer to write it down, do that here.

1. ....
2. ....
3. ....
4. ....
5. ....

Date:

How does this affirmation make you feel?

....
....
....
....

What blocks/negative beliefs are brought up for you

....
....
....
....

Thinking of each block in turn, now say:
- *Please forgive me*
- *I'm sorry*
- *Thank you*
- *I love you*

Today I am grateful for:

....
....
....

Day 78

Todays Affirmation:

Say this affirmation several times out loud with your hand on your heart looking at yourself in the mirror.

If you prefer to write it down, do that here.

1. ....
2. ....
3. ....
4. ....
5. ....

Date:

How does this affirmation make you feel?

....

....

....

....

What blocks/negative beliefs are brought up for you

....

....

....

....

Thinking of each block in turn, now say:
- *Please forgive me*
- *I'm sorry*
- *Thank you*
- *I love you*

Today I am grateful for:

....

....

....

Day 79

Todays Affirmation:

Say this affirmation several times out loud with your hand on your heart looking at yourself in the mirror.

If you prefer to write it down, do that here.

1. ....
2. ....
3. ....
4. ....
5. ....

Date:

How does this affirmation make you feel?

....

....

....

....

What blocks/negative beliefs are brought up for you

....

....

....

....

Thinking of each block in turn, now say:

- *Please forgive me*
- *I'm sorry*
- *Thank you*
- *I love you*

Today I am grateful for:

....

....

....

Day 80

Todays Affirmation:

Say this affirmation several times out loud with your hand on your heart looking at yourself in the mirror.

If you prefer to write it down, do that here.

1. ....
2. ....
3. ....
4. ....
5. ....

Date:

How does this affirmation make you feel?

....
....
....
....

What blocks/negative beliefs are brought up for you

....
....
....
....

Thinking of each block in turn, now say:

- *Please forgive me*
- *I'm sorry*
- *Thank you*
- *I love you*

Today I am grateful for:

....
....
....

Day 81

Todays Affirmation:

Say this affirmation several times out loud with your hand on your heart looking at yourself in the mirror.

If you prefer to write it down, do that here.

1. ....
2. ....
3. ....
4. ....
5. ....

Date:

How does this affirmation make you feel?

....

....

....

....

What blocks/negative beliefs are brought up for you

....

....

....

....

Thinking of each block in turn, now say:
- *Please forgive me*
- *I'm sorry*
- *Thank you*
- *I love you*

Today I am grateful for:

....

....

....

Day 82

Todays Affirmation:

Say this affirmation several times out loud with your hand on your heart looking at yourself in the mirror.

If you prefer to write it down, do that here.

1. ....
2. ....
3. ....
4. ....
5. ....

Date:

How does this affirmation make you feel?

....

....

....

....

What blocks/negative beliefs are brought up for you

....

....

....

....

Thinking of each block in turn, now say:

- *Please forgive me*
- *I'm sorry*
- *Thank you*
- *I love you*

Today I am grateful for:

....

....

....

Day 83

Todays Affirmation:

Say this affirmation several times out loud with your hand on your heart looking at yourself in the mirror.

If you prefer to write it down, do that here.

1. ....
2. ....
3. ....
4. ....
5. ....

Date:

How does this affirmation make you feel?
....
....
....
....

What blocks/negative beliefs are brought up for you
....
....
....
....

Thinking of each block in turn, now say:
- *Please forgive me*
- *I'm sorry*
- *Thank you*
- *I love you*

Today I am grateful for:
....
....
....

Day 84

Todays Affirmation:

Say this affirmation several times out loud with your hand on your heart looking at yourself in the mirror.

If you prefer to write it down, do that here.

1. ....
2. ....
3. ....
4. ....
5. ....

Date:

How does this affirmation make you feel?

....

....

....

....

What blocks/negative beliefs are brought up for you

....

....

....

....

Thinking of each block in turn, now say:
- *Please forgive me*
- *I'm sorry*
- *Thank you*
- *I love you*

Today I am grateful for:

....

....

....

Day 85

Todays Affirmation:

Say this affirmation several times out loud with your hand on your heart looking at yourself in the mirror.

If you prefer to write it down, do that here.

1. ....
2. ....
3. ....
4. ....
5. ....

Date:

How does this affirmation make you feel?

....
....
....
....

What blocks/negative beliefs are brought up for you

....
....
....
....

Thinking of each block in turn, now say:

- *Please forgive me*
- *I'm sorry*
- *Thank you*
- *I love you*

Today I am grateful for:

....
....
....

Day 86

Todays Affirmation:

Say this affirmation several times out loud with your hand on your heart looking at yourself in the mirror.

If you prefer to write it down, do that here.

1. ....
2. ....
3. ....
4. ....
5. ....

Date:

How does this affirmation make you feel?

....

....

....

....

What blocks/negative beliefs are brought up for you

....

....

....

....

Thinking of each block in turn, now say:

- *Please forgive me*
- *I'm sorry*
- *Thank you*
- *I love you*

Today I am grateful for:

....

....

....

Day 87

Todays Affirmation:

Say this affirmation several times out loud with your hand on your heart looking at yourself in the mirror.

If you prefer to write it down, do that here.

1. ....
2. ....
3. ....
4. ....
5. ....

Date:
_____

How does this affirmation make you feel?

....

....

....

....

What blocks/negative beliefs are brought up for you

....

....

....

....

Thinking of each block in turn, now say:

- *Please forgive me*
- *I'm sorry*
- *Thank you*
- *I love you*

Today I am grateful for:

....

....

....

_____

Day 88

Todays Affirmation:

Say this affirmation several times out loud with your hand on your heart looking at yourself in the mirror.

If you prefer to write it down, do that here.

1. ....
2. ....
3. ....
4. ....
5. ....

Date:

How does this affirmation make you feel?

....

....

....

....

What blocks/negative beliefs are brought up for you

....

....

....

....

Thinking of each block in turn, now say:

- *Please forgive me*
- *I'm sorry*
- *Thank you*
- *I love you*

Today I am grateful for:

....

....

....

Day 89

Todays Affirmation:

Say this affirmation several times out loud with your hand on your heart looking at yourself in the mirror.

If you prefer to write it down, do that here.

1. ....
2. ....
3. ....
4. ....
5. ....

Date:

How does this affirmation make you feel?

....
....
....
....

What blocks/negative beliefs are brought up for you

....
....
....
....

Thinking of each block in turn, now say:
- *Please forgive me*
- *I'm sorry*
- *Thank you*
- *I love you*

Today I am grateful for:

....
....
....

Day 90

Todays Affirmation:

Say this affirmation several times out loud with your hand on your heart looking at yourself in the mirror.

If you prefer to write it down, do that here.

1. ....
2. ....
3. ....
4. ....
5. ....

Date:

How does this affirmation make you feel?

....

....

....

....

What blocks/negative beliefs are brought up for you

....

....

....

....

Thinking of each block in turn, now say:

- *Please forgive me*
- *I'm sorry*
- *Thank you*
- *I love you*

Today I am grateful for:

....

....

....

How do I feel my mindset has improved over the last 30 days?

What areas do I feel I still need to work on?

Affirmations to choose from:

I accept myself unconditionally

♥ ♥ ♥ ♥ ♥

I am confident in my individuality

♥ ♥ ♥ ♥ ♥

I am deserving of happiness, love, peace, freedom, money and anything else I desire

♥ ♥ ♥ ♥ ♥

I am pure beauty

♥ ♥ ♥ ♥ ♥

I am more than a body

♥ ♥ ♥ ♥ ♥

I am open to receive

♥ ♥ ♥ ♥ ♥

I am fierce

♥ ♥ ♥ ♥ ♥

I am loved beyond comprehension

♥ ♥ ♥ ♥ ♥

I have my back

♥ ♥ ♥ ♥ ♥

I honour my inner voice

♥ ♥ ♥ ♥ ♥

I honour & respect my limitations and thank myself for the capabilities I do have

I believe in the person I dream of becoming

♥ ♥ ♥ ♥ ♥

I radiate love, peace and happiness

♥ ♥ ♥ ♥ ♥

I release the need to judge myself

♥ ♥ ♥ ♥ ♥

I walk this world with grace

♥ ♥ ♥ ♥ ♥

I can handle whatever comes my way

♥ ♥ ♥ ♥ ♥

My every step is one of courage

♥ ♥ ♥ ♥ ♥

Self-love comes to me with ease

♥ ♥ ♥ ♥ ♥

I am safe. I am supported. I am protected

♥ ♥ ♥ ♥ ♥

I choose to see things differently

♥ ♥ ♥ ♥ ♥

I choose not to take it personally

I embrace my flaws knowing that nobody is perfect

♥ ♥ ♥ ♥ ♥

I have infinite capacity for love and affection

♥ ♥ ♥ ♥ ♥

I nourish my soul and answer to my true hungers

♥ ♥ ♥ ♥ ♥

I release the need to judge myself

♥ ♥ ♥ ♥ ♥

My body is a beautiful expression of my individuality

♥ ♥ ♥ ♥ ♥

The Universe is conspiring to help me succeed

♥ ♥ ♥ ♥ ♥

My relationship with my body is one of perfect harmony

♥ ♥ ♥ ♥ ♥

I say no with ease

♥ ♥ ♥ ♥ ♥

Life is filled with joy & abundance

♥ ♥ ♥ ♥ ♥

Today, I choose me

♥ ♥ ♥ ♥ ♥

My life is a celebration of my accomplishments

♥ ♥ ♥ ♥ ♥

My mind is filled only with loving, healthy, positive and prosperous thoughts

♥ ♥ ♥ ♥ ♥

Live gives me opportunities for success and achievement in the ways I desire

♥ ♥ ♥ ♥ ♥

My voice is valuable and my opinions matter

♥ ♥ ♥ ♥ ♥

I am true

♥ ♥ ♥ ♥ ♥

I am worthy of infinite and unending compassion

♥ ♥ ♥ ♥

I believe in me

♥ ♥ ♥ ♥ ♥

I choose to stop apologizing for being me

♥ ♥ ♥ ♥ ♥

I deserve love, compassion and empathy

♥ ♥ ♥ ♥ ♥

I feel profound empathy and love for others and their own unique paths

I have come this far, and I can keep going

♥ ♥ ♥ ♥ ♥

I have the ability to overcome any challenge life gives me

♥ ♥ ♥ ♥ ♥

I have unlimited potential. Only good lies before me.

♥ ♥ ♥ ♥ ♥

I let love in

♥ ♥ ♥ ♥ ♥

I radiate confidence, self-respect and inner harmony

♥ ♥ ♥ ♥ ♥

I see my struggles as opportunities to grow and learn

♥ ♥ ♥ ♥ ♥

I trust my body's natural wisdom

♥ ♥ ♥ ♥ ♥

Love rises from my heart in the face of difficulty

♥ ♥ ♥ ♥ ♥

My body's purpose is to be love and share love

♥ ♥ ♥ ♥ ♥

My life is founded on respect for myself and others

The love within me flows through me in every situation

♥ ♥ ♥ ♥ ♥

What I give is what I receive

♥ ♥ ♥ ♥ ♥

I am good enough

♥ ♥ ♥ ♥ ♥

Abundance and love flow through me

♥ ♥ ♥ ♥ ♥

Even though I don't feel worthy right now, I know deep down that I am worthy of love, forgiveness and healing

♥ ♥ ♥ ♥ ♥

I accept compliments easily

♥ ♥ ♥ ♥ ♥

I am a beautiful person

♥ ♥ ♥ ♥ ♥

I am a radiant and joyous person

♥ ♥ ♥ ♥ ♥

I am authentic, true and expressive

♥ ♥ ♥ ♥ ♥

I am certain

♥ ♥ ♥ ♥ ♥

I am exactly where I need to be

♥ ♥ ♥ ♥ ♥

I am free to make my own choices and decisions

♥ ♥ ♥ ♥ ♥

I am loved

♥ ♥ ♥ ♥ ♥

I am not afraid to show my feelings

♥ ♥ ♥ ♥ ♥

My true self shines through today

♥ ♥ ♥ ♥ ♥

All of my decisions are inspired from inner wisdom and compassion

♥ ♥ ♥ ♥ ♥

Every part of my body radiates beauty

♥ ♥ ♥ ♥ ♥

I accept others as they are and they in turn accept me as I am

♥ ♥ ♥ ♥ ♥

I am a healer, of my own life and of others

♥ ♥ ♥ ♥ ♥

I am a work of art, cherished and admired

♥ ♥ ♥ ♥ ♥

I am balanced

♥ ♥ ♥ ♥ ♥

I am cocooned in the loving energy of the Universe

♥ ♥ ♥ ♥ ♥

I am exactly who I need to be in this moment

♥ ♥ ♥ ♥ ♥

I am growing and learning each and everyday

♥ ♥ ♥ ♥ ♥

I am moving in the best direction for me

♥ ♥ ♥ ♥ ♥

I am not my body, I am free

♥ ♥ ♥ ♥ ♥

I am powerful, beyond my wildest dreams

♥ ♥ ♥ ♥ ♥

I am wanted

♥ ♥ ♥ ♥ ♥

I am worthy of love, peace and joy

♥ ♥ ♥ ♥ ♥

I carry strength and resilience with me

♥ ♥ ♥ ♥ ♥

I consciously release the past and live only in the present

♥ ♥ ♥ ♥ ♥

I feel at peace with my appearance

♥ ♥ ♥ ♥ ♥

I have a warm and caring heart

♥ ♥ ♥ ♥ ♥

I have everything I need within myself

♥ ♥ ♥ ♥ ♥

I have the power to change my world

♥ ♥ ♥ ♥ ♥

I honour my own path

♥ ♥ ♥ ♥ ♥

I love and treasure my body

♥ ♥ ♥ ♥ ♥

I release my need for misery and suffering

♥ ♥ ♥ ♥

I stand my ground and protect myself with compassionate assertiveness

♥ ♥ ♥ ♥ ♥

I'm a diamond already. It's time to shine

♥ ♥ ♥ ♥ ♥

My body is the vehicle to my dreams

♥ ♥ ♥ ♥ ♥

My inner world creates my outer world

♥ ♥ ♥ ♥ ♥

Nothing stands in the way of my self-love. I can choose self-love now

♥ ♥ ♥ ♥ ♥

The more I practice loving myself, the more loveable I become

♥ ♥ ♥ ♥ ♥

Compassion is infinite and fully surrounds me and my life

♥ ♥ ♥ ♥ ♥

Happiness flows freely from me

I alone am whole

♥ ♥ ♥ ♥ ♥

I am a magnet for love

♥ ♥ ♥ ♥ ♥

I am abundant

♥ ♥ ♥ ♥ ♥

I am centered, peaceful, and grounded

♥ ♥ ♥ ♥ ♥

I am delightful

♥ ♥ ♥ ♥ ♥

I am exuberant and filled with love for who I am

♥ ♥ ♥ ♥ ♥

I am infinite, eternal and love

♥ ♥ ♥ ♥ ♥

I am never alone. The Universe supports me and is with me at every step

♥ ♥ ♥ ♥ ♥

I am not my mistakes

♥ ♥ ♥ ♥ ♥

I am powerful, confident, and capable of reaching all my dreams

♥ ♥ ♥ ♥ ♥

I am worthy of getting everything I want

♥ ♥ ♥ ♥ ♥

I attract wonderful people into my life

♥ ♥ ♥ ♥ ♥

I choose to be grateful for all that I have

♥ ♥ ♥ ♥ ♥

I deserve all that is good

♥ ♥ ♥ ♥ ♥

I feel completely comfortable with myself and accept myself with love, respect and appreciation

♥ ♥ ♥ ♥ ♥

I have always and will continue to always try my best; I honour this

♥ ♥ ♥ ♥ ♥

I have much to celebrate about myself and my life

♥ ♥ ♥ ♥ ♥

I have the strength to rise in the face of adversity

♥ ♥ ♥ ♥ ♥

I let go of negative self-talk

♥ ♥ ♥ ♥ ♥

I lovingly embrace all my fears

♥ ♥ ♥ ♥ ♥

I respect my accomplishments and celebrate my successes

♥ ♥ ♥ ♥ ♥

I trust in my ability to survive and thrive through any obstacle

♥ ♥ ♥ ♥ ♥

Love brings me youthfulness, energy and rejuvenates me

♥ ♥ ♥ ♥ ♥

My body, mind and soul are the picture of perfect health

♥ ♥ ♥ ♥ ♥

My life is a place of happiness and love

♥ ♥ ♥ ♥ ♥

Success is defined by my willingness to keep going

♥ ♥ ♥ ♥ ♥

The only approval I'll ever need is mine

♥ ♥ ♥ ♥ ♥

Rebecca Norton

Rebecca is the founder and director of Sense of Direction. A firm believer in life-long learning Rebecca has been interested in personal development for many years and decided to consolidate her learning by becoming a Life Coach. As a lover of the great outdoors Rebecca conducts many of her coaching sessions and events while walking. She has a vast amount of experience in training; delivering a wide variety of engaging workshops.

Contact Rebecca:

www.senseofdirection.life
www.facebook.com/RNSenseofdirection
www.linkedin.com/in/rebeccanlifecoach

Jo Outram

Jo is the founder of the Financial Fitness Club and is a Law of Attraction coach, primarily working with women in business to improve their wealth (abundance).

Contact Jo:

www.financialfitnessclub.com
www.facebook.com/financialfitnessclubs
www.linkedin.com/in/jooutram
www.instagram.com/financial_fitness_club

Other titles by Jo Outram available on Lulu Publishing & Amazon:

Wealth Journal: Change Your Money Mindset in 90 Days

Love Journal - Change Your Mindset in 90 Days And Allow Your Soulmate Into Your Life

Printed in Great Britain
by Amazon